The Second Language Learner's Handbook.

Brendan James

CONTENTS

1. About This Book and About The Author.

2. The Common European Framework of Reference For Languages.

3. Four Language Skills.

4. Parts Of Speech.

5. Be Organised.

6. ET.

7. In The Classroom.

8. Find A Good Teacher.

9. Read!!

10. Listening.

11. Speaking and Conversation Classes.

12. Writing.

13. The Actor and The Language Learner.

14. Vocabulary.

15. Homework.

16. *Intercambios*

17. Exams.

18. Subtitles.

19. Review and Memorise.

20. Mistakes Are Good!

21. Corrections.

22. Handheld Devices.

23. What Happens In The Classroom Stays In The
Classroom.

ABOUT THIS BOOK AND ABOUT THE AUTHOR

I would like to take this opportunity to thank you for buying my book and now that you have it, I hope you enjoy it. You will find that it contains lots of advice for anyone learning a second language or for anyone who is about to embark on a foreign language course. The idea came to me as a result of several years experience as an EFL teacher, my experience as a learner of the Spanish language and a third factor related to acting, which I will talk about later in this introduction. EFL stands for English as a Foreign Language and I therefore only have experience of teaching my own language, but I believe the principles are the same for any linguistic studies.

Some time ago, I began noticing that although students were being guided through the learning process in the classroom, they often were not aware of ways to improve between classes. I also noticed that I was giving the same advice repeatedly and felt that an 'instruction manual' of some sort would be very helpful. For those reasons, the idea for *The Second Language Learner's Handbook* evolved.

Although I was born in London, I now live and work in Madrid and have every intention of staying here in this wonderful sunny city. I was very happy living in England when I was younger but like a lot of people, I had the desire to visit other places and travel. One of my destinations happened to be the capital of Spain. I first came to Madrid in the summer of 2005 and immediately fell in love with this city. I knew from the moment I arrived that I wanted to live here.

A couple of years later, I left my country of birth and set up home in Spain. Soon after arriving, I enrolled on a teacher training course accredited by Cambridge University and ,after a gruelling process, I managed to pass it and become the proud owner of a CELTA certificate. CELTA is an acronym; it stands for Certificate in English Language Teaching to Adults.

Just before leaving England, I had also come to the end of several years of professional actor training in London, so I was in possession of a trained voice and I had acquired the ability to form vowel and consonant sounds correctly in order to produce *Received Pronunciation*. In my opinion, these skills are essential for any teacher, especially a trained voice, because you need to be able to use it correctly in your first class at nine in the morning when you say, 'Good morning, have you done your homework?'

and in your last class at nine in the evening when you say, 'Please do your homework!' Yes, I work long hours. The professional actor training which I undertook in London before coming to Spain combined with my experience of teaching English as a foreign language, and also my experience of learning Spanish as a second language is what convinced me that I could provide valuable advice to the *SL* (second language) learner and what led me to write this book. Had it not been for the combination of those three factors, I probably wouldn't have come up with the idea. The acting connection will be explained in more detail later in the chapter *The Actor and the Language Learner*. Hence, this book is full of tips for the *SL* learner. Some advice comes from my experience as a teacher, some comes from my experience of being a student of Spanish, some from my knowledge of acting and some is a mixture of all three with a bit of common sense thrown in for good measure.

Note: I have designed the book to be read in order as there are some explanations at the beginning which need to be read in order to understand other information later in the book. When you have finished it completely, you can re-read sections as and when you like.

Thank you once again for your interest and I wish you every success with your second language studies!

THE COMMON EUROPEAN FRAMEWORK OF REFERENCE FOR LANGUAGES

The Common European Framework of Reference for Languages (CEFR) was set up by The Council of Europe to provide a comprehensible foundation in order to design language syllabuses.

There are six levels: A1, A2, B1, B2, C1, C2.

A1 is the lowest and C2 the highest.

By typing CEFR into the search bar of your internet search engine, you will be able to find information and view a table which explains what a language learner should be able to do at each stage. It is important that you are able to identify which skills you possess by reading the short description for each level. You need to be honest with yourself and you should read the information carefully in your own language in order to avoid any confusion.

To give you an example: I have a B1 level in Spanish but I can see by reading the details in B2 that I am approaching that stage. However, I have to be honest with myself and admit that, even after several years studying, my skills at this moment in time satisfy B1 and not B2.

To reiterate: please read the details carefully and tell your teacher or the language school, where you want to study, what your CEFR level is. Your teacher and/or the school will also give you a level test which (combined with your self-evaluation) will help when choosing which course to study.

Finding your correct position in the CEFR is essential when deciding on a course of studies because you need to follow a syllabus which is not too easy, not too difficult but *challenging*!

FOUR LANGUAGE SKILLS

There are four language skills:
- Reading
- Writing
- Listening
- Speaking

I refer to these skills throughout this book so it is important to understand at the outset what these abilities mean.

- Reading: understanding fully the text you are reading and understanding the message the author intended.
- Writing: being able to convey a comprehensible message in written form; you are the author and you want the reader to understand what you want to say.

- Listening: concentrating on what you are hearing, analysing the message and forming ideas and opinions from what you have heard. This, of course, is vital in a conversation if you want to be able to respond intelligently.
- Speaking: conveying thoughts and opinions in an understandable way verbally. As this is the fastest form of communication, it is sometimes the most difficult skill to develop.

PARTS OF SPEECH

When I was at school we studied seven parts of speech. How do I know that? Because I still have my English books from those days. Nowadays, the general consensus is that there are eight parts of speech in English. The same is true for many languages but some academics insist that there are others. The more I research this subject, the more differences I find.

For simplicity, we are going to look at nine. And before you ask if a part of speech is a section of a talk given by someone to an audience; allow me to explain.

A part of speech is, quite simply, the type of word in a sentence or phrase; the word class, and they are as follows:

- NOUN - (car, house, dog, etc)

- VERB – (drive, eat, live, etc)

- ADJECTIVE - (hot, cold, big, small, etc)

- ADVERB – (loudly, badly, quickly, etc)

- PREPOSITION – (in, on, at, before, after etc)

- PRONOUN – (I, we, them, it, one, etc)

- CONJUNCTION – (but, because, and, etc)

- INTERJECTION – (Hi! Hello! Ouch! Oops! etc)

- DETERMINER – (a, the, every, etc)

Frequently, I ask my students to identify the parts of speech in a sentence. The reason I do this is to help explain some grammar, especially if there is a formula or rule to follow. It is therefore essential that you understand under which category a word falls.

Most are obvious but there are some words which change the part of speech depending on the context. It is necessary, therefore, to consult a good dictionary when studying grammar. You might find it a good idea to dissect words which have several different parts of speech in order to understand them better. Draw a diagram to give yourself an exploded view - a quick visual reference, to help comprehend the most complicated words more easily. You could also design a diagram to show the different types of adverbs and nouns for instance. Go and do some research - it's fun!

BE ORGANISED

It is not uncommon to see students arrive at class clutching their books along with piles of loose papers. This a good sign because it means they have their notes with them. But a problem surfaces when they make a mistake in class and I ask them to review some grammar, an item of vocabulary or a basic question formation which we had studied beforehand. A frantic search ensues involving a never ending flicking through of papers. Very often, they are unable to locate the required notes and then I have to resort to explaining again. This is especially frustrating because an opportunity to guide students towards *learner autonomy* using their own notes from a previous class has been lost. What's more, all of this searching and explaining again takes up valuable class time.

The advice here, then, is to buy a folder BEFORE

you start your course and file away photocopies and handouts into an organised system immediately. You will then be able to locate your notes more easily and more quickly. Divide your folder into sections that are user-friendly for you!

As a student who is learning Spanish, I also have to be organised. I review my notes, summarise them and then transfer them into a notebook. Most handouts and photocopies are A4 size but my notebook is A5 which enables me to do two things. Firstly, it is small enough to carry around and take with me when I am going to an *intercambio* (see chapter 16) or a Spanish class. Secondly, it helps me to be concise when summarizing, due to its small size. Another important consideration to be taken into account when studying is to throw away or, better still, recycle the paper which contains your original notes.

Once you have reviewed them and they have been entered comprehensibly into your notebook, THROW AWAY (or recycle) the original ones. Imagine how refreshed you will feel when you realise that your notes are neatly organised in an A5 size notebook and that the original ones, which you scribbled down hurriedly in class, will go to help produce new paper based products!

If you have followed my advice, you will be thinking of racing to the nearest stationery shop - but not so fast! There are some other things you should consider buying - highlighter pens. Imagine this scenario. You have worked very hard to organise and collate your work and now you have a book full of handwritten notes. There lies another problem. All of the pages look the same and it could off-putting. My advice, therefore, is to colour code them to help you when a quick review is needed but also for a more aesthetically pleasing view in general. You could also try your hand at drawing colourful illustrations and diagrams which are particularly useful for a quick review but also break up the monotony when wading through page after page of handwritten notes.

By the way, highlighter pens are also essential in class. Let's say you have to do an exercise which requires that you have to distinguish between parts of speech from a chart full of words. By using different colours to highlight the part of speech, you will have an instant visual record of your work and eliminate the need to draw several columns in a page in your notebook.

I have mentioned above what I believe are the basic essentials for any language learner.

Now, if you so desire, you may poodle off to the nearest stationery shop.

ET

What does *ET* stand for? - I hear you ask. *ET* was, of course, the title of a very popular film about a lovable, friendly little alien and his visit to earth. But in the world of language learning, it stands for *Exposure Time* - the amount of time you are receptive to a language - be it from reading, listening, speaking or writing. The quantity of time you are exposed to your second language will greatly affect your success and it is therefore necessary to be aware of how high or low your *ET* is.

In order to explain further, I would like to have a look at some numbers. In case you were unaware, I can tell you that there are 168 hours in one week. Let's say that the average person sleeps for around 56 hours and we are left with 112 hours of '*awake time*'. And if we say, for argument's sake, that we spend another 12 hours in the bathroom, in the toilet or doing solitary or personal things, you will see that we have reached a nice round number of 100. Let's call this your *Target Time* or *TT*.

I haven't conducted a scientific study in order to reach this number but I think it is fair to say that the average person is probably exposed to language for around that many hours in a week. If you are reading this and you decide to carry out a scientific study to counteract my claims, might I suggest that you do something more interesting, like learning a second language for example. Jokes aside, 100 is also an easy number to use due to its relationship with percentages and it is an easy number to remember. So, if you agree with me so far, we will proceed.

When growing up, you were probably completely unaware that you were learning your mother tongue but due to the constant exposure from your parents, siblings, relatives, friends, neighbours, television, radio, comics, books, breakfast cereal boxes, shampoo containers and so on, you learned quickly and were able to communicate from a very young age. You probably weren't articulate when you started school but you would have been able to communicate reasonably well. Reaching this same level of exposure in your second language is almost impossible to do, even if you live in a country where that language is spoken. I am an Englishman living in Spain, so I have personal experience of this. *My* biggest problem, and the reason it is taking me so long to learn Spanish, is because of low *ET*. It's probably a good moment to remind you that *ET* stands for exposure time to a second language and is not an abbreviation for a medical condition! I have a contract which dictates that I have to work 34 classroom hours teaching English. This figure fluctuates but, on average, including class preparation and correcting time, I probably work for around 40 hours a week. I am therefore left with around 60 hours of *TT*. My next problem is that I have a TV service from a very well known telephone supplier in Spain which, at the touch of a button, allows me to watch programmes in English. I can also record programmes with this service and change the language accordingly. Sometimes, I am so tired after a long day teaching that all I want to do is chill out in front of the TV and be a couch potato. To explain further, I spend the best part of my evening zapping from one American series to another, watching shows like Top Gear and Wheeler Dealers or switching between CNN and BBC world news! The advice here is NOT to follow my example but instead, be aware of your level of *ET* and increase it as much as possible. Please don't feel demoralised if your *ET* is very low. The point of this chapter is to make you aware of the possibilities and not to set impossible targets. So, don't panic! Just do the best you can. The number 100 is easy to remember, so try and keep it in your mind and ask yourself at the end of the week how close you came to reaching it.

If you are enrolled on a course of studies for one academic year and you attend two one and a half hour classes per week, you will manage to accumulate a grand total of 3 hours or 3% of your *TT*. Quite clearly, this is not enough. With homework, however, your *ET* could go up by another 2 or 3 hours and reach an amazing 6 hours. Wow! I jest. I think it is clear to see that this is still not enough; you need to think of ways of increasing this figure. Keep a record of the time you devote to your *SL* learning and try to increase it every week. There are two things you can do right now to help raise your *ET*. Change the language on your computer and your mobile phone. There is a third thing you can do when you next go to the bank; change the language on the cash machine. However, If you become confused and withdraw copious amounts of cash or transfer your entire life savings to another person's account, please don't blame me; I am only trying to help.

So there you have a few to get you started but you need more. I can give you some ideas and tell you about my methods for practising but you can also invent some ways yourself.

I often hear students say that they don't have very much free time and therefore they can't devote much time to practising. But bearing in mind that I have experience as a teacher and as a language learner, I always have an answer for almost all excuses. Some students say they spend several hours in the car commuting and that it is impossible to practise while driving. Wrong! When I came to Spain, I brought with me a selection of CDs which I had collected from a newspaper back in England. At first, I found them interesting and helpful as a listening exercise but after a while I grew tired of listening to the same discs time and time again, so I needed a new safe way of practising while alone in my car. Telephoning while driving is prohibited here in Spain, so that wasn't an option. And then one day it occurred to me that practice was all around! Allow me to explain. I have noticed that a lot of my students have problems reciting the English alphabet. This type of activity is seen as something that a young child should do, and not an adult. However, it is vital that you are able to pronounce the letters of your *SL*. It is also essential that you are able to recognize the sound of each letter when someone is spelling something. Without wanting to boast, I can recite the Spanish alphabet easily. My secret? I read the number plates of the other road users. In Spain, there are still some old

number plates on older cars but the modern
system consists of four numbers followed by
three letters. When I see the characters, I say
them aloud. This is also good numerical practice.
The four numbers I mentioned earlier can be
practised by reading each one separately or two,
three or four together. Imagine a registration
plate such as 1234 ABC. I can practise by saying
one, two, three, four or twelve, thirty-four or one
hundred and twenty-three or one thousand, two
hundred and thirty-four. I can also say A for
apple, B for boat, C for coat as a way of
'extracting' vocabulary from my mind. The list
of ways is endless. You just need a little bit of
creativity. Read aloud road signs, speed limit
signs, shop signs and so on. I think you will
agree that there are many ways of increasing
your *ET*, even when you are alone in the car. At
this point I would like to point out that if this
affects your concentration while driving, please

don't do it for the sake of *your* safety and that of the other drivers around you. As I have experience of doing this myself, I can report that it is a safe method for me. In fact, I find having a conversation more distracting! You have been warned.

Another useful exercise is to complete your shopping list in your second language. If you live in the country where the language is spoken, you will see the words on the products in the shops, but if you don't, it is still a good exercise to do. Take a look around you now. Can you put a name to all the objects that you can see? If you can't, look them up in a dictionary and label them. This is not a good idea if you are on a bus or train at this moment and you feel the urge to put a label on the cap of the person sitting opposite you. OK, so I'm joking, but I think you get the idea.

All of these techniques are increasing your *ET* because you are spending time thinking in your chosen second language. Make a list of *SL* activities and calculate the time needed to accomplish them. Change the language on your TV, go to the cinema and watch films in original version, arrange an *intercambio* (see chapter 16), read in your second language, write a diary, listen to radio and so on. The onus is on you to raise your *ET* so *you* must be the person to design your weekly second language learning timetable. Put a list on the fridge with a column on the right hand side to record the time spent on each activity and add up the times at the end of the week. Are you close to the number 100 yet?

One way of reaching maximum *TT* would be to live in a country where your chosen second language is spoken with a host family, for a week or two. Submerging yourself in this way would produce good results but you must be brave and go alone, and not with a friend! It is important to have zero communication with friends during this time in order to get near maximum TT. If you decide to do this, leave your shyness at home and speak to everyone you meet. Ask complete strangers in the street for directions, even if you know where you are going. Read newspapers, read advertisements in public places, listen to music while walking along the street, listen to the local people speaking. This drastic way of raising ET is effective but it can be difficult to be away from friends and family and that is why I suggest only one or two weeks.

Remember: the list of different ways to increase ET is almost endless so there really is no excuse for not practising your second language and let's face it; you shouldn't be looking for excuses anyway because you want to learn! And if you don't have the desire to learn but are obligated to because of your job perhaps, just think how impressed your friends, colleagues and family will be when they see you communicating in a second language. And if that isn't enough encouragement, I don't know what is!

IN THE CLASSROOM

I'm going to be blunt … Be prepared to work hard, study diligently and communicate enthusiastically in your class. A classroom is not a place to rest and relax! OK … Now that I have got that off my chest, I will proceed.

Bringing energy into the classroom is vital. You should arrive with the intention of interacting with your classmates (or with your teacher if you have a one to one class). To learn a language, you need to be proactive and put energy into the process. Don't rely on osmosis, rely on yourself!

When I undertook my CELTA training course, I was taught many things. One of which, I use in every class I give. One of my teachers had a twenty second rule. The rule was simple. The students have to start speaking within the first twenty seconds of entering the class. I believe the advantages are twofold. Firstly, the students make full use of the time they are paying for. Secondly, it is an opportunity for the teacher to energise the students who sometimes arrive tired after a hard day at work. At times such as these, the teacher's job is to remind the students that they have not come to class to rest or relax; they have come to learn, even if they are tired. Another important thing to remember, which might seem obvious, is to speak in the language of your class. In some of my classes, I have to remind students to communicate in English. I understand that it is difficult to speak in another language when your thoughts are connected to your mother tongue but it is very important that you don't speak in your own language for two reasons. One, you need to practise speaking in your *SL*. Two, there are other students in the class who are paying money to listen to their *SL*. If everybody arrives in class with the intention of speaking only in the language they are studying, the success rate will be higher in the long term and all students will feel satisfied with the training. In elementary classes, it is sometimes necessary for the teacher to speak in the students' language to explain something but remember that your teacher may not speak your language.

Another thing you should not do as a student in any classroom is use smart phones for any purpose other than a dictionary. There are many popular messaging services which people like to use nowadays and being in touch with family and friends 24/7 seems to be the norm but during the study period students must be focused on their studies. In the past, in my country, it wasn't unusual to see a *swear box* in public places. A swear box is basically a money box with a slot for coins to be dropped into should a person use a bad word. They were used as a gimmick and people used to buy them as holiday souvenirs. I have a similar system in my classroom. I have a tin with a slot in the top as a warning to students that if they speak in Spanish they have to insert some money. I bought it a couple of years ago and stuck a label on the front with the words NO SPANISH. I have since had to add NO TELEPHONES, NO INSTANT MESSAGING and several other important 'prohibitions'. If I were strict and insisted on them putting money into the tin, I would be able to afford exotic holidays every year but, sadly, it remains empty. I realise that, from time to time, an important call might have to be answered but, apart from that, mobile phones should not be used. *Thank you*.

My advice before entering your class is the following: *'change the chip'*. Remind yourself of your objectives and why you have decided to study. Enter in a receptive mood ready to communicate immediately. Start thinking in your second language on the way to your class. If you come to one of my classes, I expect nothing less, even if you are exhausted!

Apologies in advance.

FIND A GOOD TEACHER

Several years ago in England there was an advertising campaign which stated that you never forget a good teacher. The advertisement consisted of people saying the name of a teacher from their school days that they would always remember. For the record, I would like to add the name of the person I will never forget: Mr Moore, my French teacher. Why? Because he knew how to do his job with expertise. Sadly, Mr Moore died at a very young age and I am sorry to say that my studies suffered afterwards because his replacement was nowhere near the same calibre. Therefore, finding a good teacher is essential.

In the world of second language learning this is sometimes not an easy task. I have chosen to teach because I feel it is my vocation; I realised I had the required abilities to educate and I intend

34

to do the job for as long as I'm physically able to. I also accept that I will have to improve my teaching skills as I face new challenges and to learn new things and adapt to new methods. My intention, therefore, is to help people learn a second language. Some foreign language teachers are actually people who want to learn a language themselves and go to a specific country where it is spoken in order to improve their own skills. Normally, the only work available to these people is language teaching. It is important to understand that some might have the abilities, but some might not. The golden rule here is: if they don't measure up to *your* 'Mr Moore',find another one.

A couple of years ago, I contacted a Spanish teacher who was advertising her services on a well known website. The classes were very cheap and the first one was free. It sounded like a good idea and, besides, I didn't have to pay for the first one, so I wasn't going to lose anything. How wrong I was! Taking into account the time required to get to the class, I lost over four hours of my life to one of the most talkative people I have ever met! However, I did learn one useful Spanish phrase so it wasn't a total loss but whenever I use it, and believe me, it is very commonly used when speaking Spanish, I am reminded of those four painful hours! It transpired that she was not in fact Spanish. She was married to a Spaniard and she spoke the language perfectly but she didn't have the first idea how to teach and, as a result, she spent the first and second hour speaking about her life and the problems she was facing because she didn't have a job. Her classes (I use the word *classes* lightly) were purely to earn a bit of money to get by. I mentioned that she spoke for two hours; this is because I felt sorry for her and decided to have a second class to see if in fact

36

she could teach. Sadly, she couldn't, so I didn't have a third.

My advice here, then, is the following. Ask your teacher if he or she has a qualification to teach. Maybe they are only going to be in the country for a short time to improve their second language skills but they should at least have had some form of training. If a person is going to take your time and money, make sure he or she knows what they are doing.

Training is important for many reasons. The teachers I had when undertaking my CELTA course where all experts in their field and I learned a lot from them. One thing I learned about was *TTT*. This stands for *Teacher Talking Time*. In the past, teachers probably felt the need to talk a lot but over the years teaching methods have changed and, as a result, *TTT* must be kept low. At times, it is absolutely necessary for a teacher to speak and explain things but *TTT* must be kept to a minimum.

To summarise: if your teacher talks too much, find another one.

READ!!

This Might seem obvious, but reading is essential if you want to master your second language. Over the years, I have given many courses based on syllabuses designed by linguists. In my opinion, the resultant course books are extremely beneficial to the second language learner because they are very thorough, owing to the fact that they have originated from people who have language learning expertise, and that they are designed to provide a comprehensive understanding of a foreign language. Glancing at the contents page, you will see that many aspects are covered. However, there are things that aren't taught. It would be almost impossible to cover all parts of a language in one book which is designed for one academic year.

So how do we learn colloquial language?

Idioms? Fixed expressions? And if you are familiar with the English language, how do we learn the dreaded multi-word verbs, more commonly known as phrasal verbs? The answer has one syllable; read. I could end this chapter here because I am sure you will agree that I am stating the obvious but you would be surprised by how many *SL* learners do not read on a regular basis. Ask your teacher for advice or do some research on the internet to find books suitable for your level in line with the CEFR.

In today's world, more than ever before, everybody seems to be communicating in written form. I used to speak a lot by telephone in the past but nowadays I very rarely communicate verbally, unless I am with the person I want to speak to of course. The world also works at a faster place and responses are required more quickly than ever before.

By reading regularly, and understanding fully

what is being read, the *SL* learner will be far better equipped to deal with the rising quantity of electronic messaging. This method of communication could be between friends where attention to detail might not be that important but if the communication is from a potential employer, a client, or your boss, understanding what is being said and being able to respond intelligently with correct grammar and correct spelling is fundamental.

Another good reason to read regularly is to become accustomed to prepositions. Frequently, I am asked by my students if there are any rules which govern this problematic part of speech. It would be great if I could reply that, yes there are and it's very easy to memorise them; but it is not that simple. On hearing their requests, I hand out photocopies containing common prepositions and what they are used with, exercises for verbs and adjectives and their dependent prepositions and other helpful worksheets. Later, when they hand in an essay, I notice the same mistakes. Reading will help to eradicate this problem because your eyes are exposed to the language, thus avoiding the need to memorise endless lists of information. It is important, however, to fully understand what you are reading. If possible, buy a book or magazine that has comprehension exercises. I have found from my experience of learning Spanish that I sometimes read a text and don't pay complete attention to it. I think I understand because I recognise most of the words as I skim over the article but, when I have to answer comprehension questions, I realise that I haven't understood it as well as I should have done and, therefore, have to scan the text more carefully. It is during this second or third scan that I notice more of the structure of the language and the usage of prepositions.

While we are on the subject of prepositions, I would like to mention one more thing. I have an excellent book which is designed specifically for learners of the English language. It is a dictionary of collocations. By flicking through it, one begins to notice the numerous combinations available. As a native speaker of English, I don't need to memorise the contents of this dictionary because of the exposure to the English language I have had during my lifetime but I do use it for reference purposes.

I hope you are convinced of the need to read, read and read some more but just in case you are not, I would like to point out one more thing. Reading is vital if you want to enrich your range of vocabulary. Any writer worth their salt will avoid repeating words as much as possible. This may involve reconstructing a sentence, using pronouns or searching for synonyms so that you, the reader, can enjoy the text. It is not unusual for an *SL* learner to spend more time with his or her head buried in a dictionary than in a book but I'm afraid this is all part of the process. As you progress, you will learn the meaning of more words and you will also be able to work out the meaning from the context. But that doesn't happen overnight and for that reason it is necessary to read as much as possible.

I mentioned earlier that writers worth their salt will avoid repetition and then I go and repeat the words *read* and *reading* several times. The word subliminal comes to mind…

LISTENING

Improving listening abilities is one of the most problematic parts of learning a language, in my opinion. Difficulties arise because you have to receive a lot of information through your ears in a foreign language at a speed that you may not be comfortable with. This skill can be improved by doing listening comprehension exercises in class but also by doing activities at home. When I first arrived in Spain, I couldn't understand anything. I also found it difficult to pick up any of the language at first because of the big differences between the way that Spanish people and English people communicate. When talking about sport or politics, Spanish people can become quite animated. At first, I thought they were angry with each other and that the normal discussions they were having were displays of rage. But I learned, little by little, due to my regular exposure to the language that, quite simply, they communicate differently to the way my countrymen speak. I have only learned this fact because of my exposure to the language and, as a result, my listening skills have improved. However, this process has taken a long time and I expect a lot more time to pass before I fully understand everything.

You have to bear in mind how quickly you need to learn. In my case for, example, I am not in a particular hurry because I can work without using Spanish. However, if your job depends on your second language, it will be necessary to improve listening skills faster. In my experience, the level of the four skills in a class can vary enormously. Some students speak very well, possibly because they have channelled their energy into this ability for many years, but understand very little. On the other hand, there are students who are perhaps shy and don't speak very much but understand almost everything. After completing a listening exercise I usually ask them to give me an approximation of how much they understood by using a percentage. The results are often very surprising with some students who have very good speaking and writing abilities admitting to having only understood 40 or 50% of the exercise. If you fall into this category, you should ask the teacher, if he or she hasn't already done so, to pre-teach some vocabulary from the exercise before you listen to it. That way, you will be able to understand more words and, as a result, follow the gist of the exercise. Some students don't like to be pre-taught vocabulary because they want to test themselves without any prior knowledge, so it can be difficult for the teacher to find the right balance in a class with different levels. The onus, therefore, is on the student to improve this skill

47

by doing as many exercises as possible outside the classroom.

I have tried various methods which work for me: Songs, dictation, documentaries, radio and short videos on the internet. Songs are a good resource for improving listening skills but I have found it easier to find the lyrics and study the words beforehand. When you have understood the meaning of the song you can play it at home or in the car and sing along. By singing along to the song, you are also practising pronunciation. Try to copy the singer as close as you can as a way of pronouncing better and reducing your accent. I always sing while driving but if you prefer to sing in the shower, that's fine by me.

I have also found dictation exercises very helpful. You can do this with a private teacher or with a friend, provided that the friend is a native speaker or someone with a very high level in the language you are studying. It is important

48

during this type of exercise that a sentence is read in its entirety and repeated several times if necessary, and not word by word. If you think of one sentence as one thought, you need to train your mind to understand the complete meaning and not just the words. Also, the student should type the words into a computer and delete as necessary thus avoiding an unsightly mess of mistakes on a piece of paper.

Watch documentaries. These types of films are very useful because you have a visual display of the vocabulary the narrator is using and the dialogue is delivered slowly with longish gaps so that you can understand what has been said before you are moved on to the next scene. In chapter 18, entitled *Subtitles*, I talk more about television and films but, where documentaries are concerned, you should not rely on subtitles unless you have a basic elementary level.

You can of course also listen to the radio but this

may not be the best listening comprehension exercise. It is, however, a worthwhile exercise in the sense that you are hearing the sounds of the language and intonation and let's not forget that any form of *ET* is better than no *ET*.

Another exercise that I do to improve my Spanish listening skills is to find a short video on the internet which lasts for 10 to 15 minutes. With a pen and piece of paper I listen and record all the words I have heard and understood. I then replay the video and complete the same exercise, each time adding more words. After listening several times I am generally able to fill in any gaps of missing information using my knowledge of Spanish grammar. Sometimes, however, (and this occasionally happens to me in my own language if the speaker isn't speaking clearly) I simply cannot understand a word or a part of a sentence. On those occasions, I ask a Spanish speaking friend to listen and help me.

By the way, in case you hadn't realised, if you do this exercise with a 15 minute video and replay it four times, you will have added an hour to your *ET*!

I have outlined a few examples above which have helped me. I hope they help you.

SPEAKING AND CONVERSATION CLASSES

I have just checked in my Oxford English Dictionary and I can confirm that a conversation is, and I quote, *a spoken exchange of news and ideas between people*.

In my experience as a teacher, I have come across students who are very talkative and are able to speak for a very long time in English without the need for a break. However, depending on their level, they can make a lot of mistakes which need to be corrected. I have also found from experience that some of these students have difficulty understanding the English language and compensate by speaking a lot. This is great news because it means they are able to express themselves verbally on many different topics but two problems arise. Firstly, if the student doesn't allow the teacher to speak, there will be no way of correcting. Secondly, an opportunity for the student to listen to and practise with a native speaker has been lost. If you fall into this category, try to organise your thoughts into neat little packages and construct paragraphs in your mind rather like you do when you are writing something. The gaps between these *paragraphs* will enable the teacher to correct you if he or she feels it necessary, or continue, or ask a question.

The same approach should apply in a conversation class. It is important to remember that every student attending this type of class wants to practise conversing and not just practise listening. If you deliver a monologue, your classmate will not be able to talk and will feel deflated. I agree that it is important to practise speaking as much of possible but let's not forget that we want to learn to communicate, and not just speak.

Talking at length and not listening to other people's opinions is the job of politicians, isn't it?

WRITING

I am sure you will have realised by reaching this point in the book, that I enjoy writing. In fact, I always have. In the past, I used to write as a hobby. My favourite pastime was summarising plays and stories. I have always enjoyed discovering words in the dictionary and finding synonyms and antonyms in my Thesaurus. When I am writing, I like to use all my skills to produce a final result which I am personally pleased with and one which I hope you, the reader, will enjoy.

For me, writing is a pleasure and I enjoy the experience from start to finish. So, writing in my second language should be just as pleasurable, right? Wrong!

Producing written work in Spanish is a completely different activity. My creativity is the same and my ideas flow but I become blocked because I have to think about grammar, vocabulary and the overall sense. I am never sure whether it has a *Spanish flavour* or not. In English, I think about how to make a text more colourful but, in Spanish, I struggle with the basics.

Unfortunately, this lack of confidence when writing in my second language will remain this way until I have practised time and time again. Just like when I was at school in England, I have to make mistakes and learn from them.

One way of improving writing abilities is to read more and pay attention to the way texts are constructed. Look for common phrases and *'chunks'* of language that you can, to use a computing term, *'copy and paste'* into your texts. If you want to produce good work, you need to convey your ideas but through the second language you have chosen to study. A teacher is necessary in order for this skill to flourish. You need a professional to check your work, correct it and explain the problematic areas. You can also ask your teacher if it has the *'flavour'* required to convince the reader it was written by a native speaker.

There are many other ways of practising this skill. One is to set up a writing exchange with a friend or colleague. Agree at the outset how your exchange is going to work and start sending each other messages. I have done this by email but nowadays there are umpteen ways of practising this. You can decide to correct the text you receive and return it or take your mobile device to your next meeting with your friend or colleague and explain in person. My advice here is to keep the communications at an informal level in order to avoid the need for complicated explanations.

This chapter deals with the fourth and last language skill and I think it is a good moment to remind you of the other three: reading, listening, speaking and how important it is to develop all of these skills at the same pace.

Practise all four skills regularly and you will notice improvements. Don't rush the process; take your time and enjoy the experience; strive for a good level in all abilities and use each of them to complement the others.

THE ACTOR AND THE LANGUAGE
LEARNER

For the record, I am still learning Spanish; I have
been for several years and I fully intend to do so
until I am fluent and, even then, I will continue
to maintain my level. That's what I call
determination! Fortunately, I really enjoy
learning and practising my second language and
I am happy with my progress. There are times,
however, when I speak better than others.
Sometimes I become blocked and I am unable to
string a sentence together, it depends on the day.
I now have a good working knowledge of
Spanish and can get by in most everyday
situations; so you can imagine how I felt one day
just before the Christmas holidays when I was
completely unable to communicate with a
colleague about a work related issue and had to
rely on my mother tongue to get through the

conversation (my colleague is bilingual, by the way) On the way home, I was trying to understand why I had had such difficulties in communicating with a colleague that I had known for many years. I wasn't feeling nervous, I wasn't particularly tired; granted I was feeling stressed because of the end of year report writing but I couldn't work out why. When I reached home, I took a beer from the fridge to drown my sorrows. As I took the first gulp, I suddenly realised what the problem was. It was my *eureka* moment! Allow me to explain. Having been involved in the world of acting for many years as an amateur and latterly as a professional, I have attended many many rehearsals, some good and some bad. Being a hardworking, conscientious person, I have always tried my best. On occasions, however, I hadn't had the time to look at my script and the rehearsals that followed were generally the worst.

My first acting performance was in 1997. After the play, my sister came up to me and told me that she was amazed that I had managed to remember so many lines. I am not sure what I said to her at the time but the fact is that I remembered them because I had spent a long time studying them, memorising them and practising them. The average rehearsal period for an amateur production is around seven weeks (far shorter for a professional production) For those seven weeks, I went everywhere with my script, I took it with me in my car and glanced at it while waiting for traffic lights to change from red to green, I took it with me to bed and I even took it to the bathroom. Why? Because at the time of the performance, an actor needs to be able to walk and talk as the character he is playing and be able to listen to and respond to the other actors. When the play is finished, the script is filed away on the bookshelf as a souvenir, but it's interesting that several weeks later I would still be able to recite most of the words I had memorised. But if I were to walk on stage now and try to recreate a role from several years ago, it would be almost impossible. Language learning is similar. Your script is your grammar book; the notes in your script are the notes in your notebook. And although you don't have the pressure of having to memorise all the grammar in a short period of time, you must make your learning process a regular part of your life. You must take it everywhere with you. What I mean by this is that you need to have access to the language as much as possible. Nowadays, we can carry almost unlimited information in our smart phones and tablets, so there is no excuse.

If you find that you are in a situation where you are having difficulties communicating, try to analyse what went wrong. Maybe you were unable to remember some vocabulary or perhaps a verb conjugation or it could be that you just couldn't remember which part of grammar to choose. Whatever the cause, you should identify it and go back to your books and locate the part of the language that was causing you trouble. An actor who has had a bad rehearsal will automatically go back to his script and locate the problematic area. Review your notes or read grammar explanations or look up the vocabulary necessary.

Problems encountered with vocabulary can be easily overcome by reading more. When an author writes something, he or she is aware of the need to avoid repetition and, therefore, will use synonyms, pronouns or simply reconstruct the sentence in order to produce another way of conveying the meaning of the passage. A lot of synonyms can also be learned by investing in a Thesaurus. I have one which I bought many years ago. The pages are yellowing and, in some cases, falling out but I still use it when I am writing. A Thesaurus provides synonyms and antonyms which will serve as a valuable tool to the second language learner when communicating both verbally and in written form. When you are speaking and you can't bring to mind the word you are searching for, you can switch to a synonym and continue communicating. If an actor can't remember his lines during a performance, he will resort to paraphrasing and will use different vocabulary from that which is in the script in order to tell the story.

But remember, just like the actor reviewing his script, you will need to consult all of your study aids regularly if you want to succeed. And even when you are speaking fluently, it is essential that you include regular practice into your day to day life in order to maintain and improve your level.

Now, you may applaud.

VOCABULARY

When I first started studying Spanish, I can remember making long lists of vocabulary in alphabetical order with the English word beside the Spanish word. To a certain extent, this works, especially when you are just starting out. However, as you progress you should attempt to leave your native language behind and just register newly learned vocabulary without its translation.

Another important point to make here is to record vocabulary in categories and not alphabetically. The secret behind remembering new words is to see them several times, understand the meaning and commit them to memory. This can be done by making alphabetical lists with translations but I have found it more useful to use a category system. It's important to remember that, ultimately, you want to be able to communicate without resorting to your notebook as soon as humanly possible. By listing new words in categories, you will find it easier to remember the word. For instance, if I were learning English vocabulary and I wanted to remember the words *sink* and *basin*, I would find it easier to identify the meaning of *basin* if I were to list it under the category of *bathroom* rather than in an alphabetical list. Imagine that I decide to review my vocabulary. If I couldn't remember the meaning of *basin*, I am sure, by a process of elimination, I would be able to work it out. Similarly, if I record *sink* under *Kitchen*, I learn the word and I'm also able to differentiate between *basin* and *sink*. This system also forces the student to consult the dictionary if the meaning cannot be deduced, which increases *ET*. Although vocabulary should be recorded in categories, the categories should be in alphabetical order for quick reference. I use an A5 notebook for Spanish vocabulary. I use the left hand page and leave the right hand page blank. The reason for this is to allow for an extra category to be inserted should it be required or simply to add more words from the left hand page. Remember to also include a contents page.

An example of an alphabetical list of categories is as follows:

AEROPLANES AND AIRPORTS, ANIMALS, BANKS, BICYCLES, BIRDS, BODY, CALENDAR, CARS, CINEMA, CLOTHES, COLOURS, COMPUTERS, COUNTRIES AND NATIONALITIES, DECIMALS AND FRACTIONS, DOMESTIC APPLIANCES, DRINK, EDUCATION, FAMILY, FISH, FLOWERS, FOOD, FRUIT, FURNITURE, HEALTH, HOBBIES, HOSPITAL, HOTEL, HOUSE, ILLNESS, INSECTS, JOBS, LAW, MONEY, MOTORCYCLES, MUSIC, NUMBERS, PUBLIC TRANSPORT, SHOPPING, SPORT, THEATRE, TOOLS, VEGETABLES, VEHICLES, WEATHER.

My next advice is to review vocabulary regularly and not to add lots of words to any one list too quickly. It is common knowledge that we need to break down most tasks into bite size chunks. Imagine trying to eat your dinner in one gulp; it's impossible. If you add too many new words, you could end up with something quite daunting which is not visually pleasing and therefore difficult to absorb.

Vocabulary is very important for the simple reason that if you can't remember the correct grammar, you can still communicate and get what you want. If I were to walk into a shop in Spain, for instance, without the slightest knowledge of Spanish grammar and say 'Buenos días, Pan, mantequilla y queso, por favor,' I would be able to go home and make myself a cheese sandwich, thus fulfilling my aim.

I am not an advocate of people who wish to communicate in that basic way but at the beginning, vocabulary can help a great deal, especially if you are learning Spanish which has more verb conjugations than I have had hot dinners! … or cheese sandwiches.

HOMEWORK

Do your homework! … End of chapter.

OK, I jest, but seriously, there are several reasons
why your teacher will give you homework. One
is to enable you to practise the language you
have been studying in class, in the comfort of
your own home, without any distractions. A
second reason is to increase your *ET*. A typical
course in the academy where I teach runs from
October to June and consists of two 90 minute
classes per week which comes to a grand total of
3 hours. Do you remember the 100 hours of *TT*?
It doesn't take a rocket scientist to calculate that
3 hours is a short period of time. So this second
reason is an attempt by the teacher to force you
to increase your *ET*. And before you start
thinking that your teacher is cruel for robbing
you of your free time, it is, in fact, the sign of a

good teacher who is committed to helping and guiding you through the learning process. And let's not forget, especially in the case of writing exercises, that your teacher has to give up a lot of his or her free time correcting your work. So remember - the more homework teachers give you, the more they love you!

A third reason is to reduce the gaps between classes. If you have a class on Monday and another one on Wednesday, forty six and a half hours will go by without any *ET*. But if you do your homework on Tuesday, for example, the gaps of non *ET* will be shorter. Clever, isn't it?

So … Do your homework! … End of chapter.

INTERCAMBIOS

When I first arrived in Spain, I participated in
several different types of *intercambios*. An
intercambio is a language exchange between two
or several people. They are a great way to
practise conversational skills and also a great
way to meet new people. I didn't make any life
long friends but I got myself invited to several
functions and social engagements, which are a
godsend when you first arrive in a foreign
country and are missing your friends and
family.

There are many different ways of becoming
involved in *intercambios*. I have experience of this
type of activity as a second language learner and
my experience comes from what I have done in
Madrid but I am sure the same applies to other
cities around the world.

My first *intercambio* was in a large bar in the

centre of Madrid. I noticed an advertisement on a website which encouraged people to get together and I decided to go along. I arrived, entered the venue and encountered what I can only describe as a throng. I managed to squeeze my way to the bar, I bought myself a drink and then returned to the main door where there were fewer people. I could tell instantly that I wasn't going to enjoy myself so I decided to finish my drink and leave. However, there were a couple of Spanish girls standing near me who were also not particularly impressed by the huge crowd of people, judging by the look on their faces. We struck up a conversation and, due to the noise level, we agreed to find somewhere quieter. We left shortly after. The girls turned out to be teachers who wanted to improve their English level, so we swapped email addresses and met again several times.

I can count the number of occasions I have been

to organised *intercambios* on one hand simply because I don't like large crowds of people. This type of function is my least favourite mainly because, in my opinion, it is difficult to hear anything due to the hubbub which is created by so many people chatting at the same time in one place. I found it particularly difficult to hear what the other person was saying to me unless he or she shouted at close range into one of my ears.

On the other hand, if your intention is to find a partner or meet friends as well as learn the language, then this is probably for you because it is less intimidating and more relaxed and there are usually a diverse range of people. But remember, this type of event is noisy....you have been warned!

My favourite type of *intercambio* is a one to one meeting in person where two people meet and take it in turns to practise their chosen language.

I have fond memories of those early days in Madrid when I used to meet various people for a language exchange. I like to refer to that period as my *'serviette days'*. Allow me to explain. The meetings generally took place in a quiet bar (difficult to find in Madrid, I can tell you!) and would involve sitting opposite your fellow *SL* learner. You agree to split the meeting so that you speak for half the time in your language and the rest in theirs. In any bar in Spain, you will find a dispenser of some description containing small serviettes. Sometimes, it is necessary to explain something and the only way is to write it down. Being a forgetful person at times, I never used to remember to take a notebook, so I used serviettes instead. I also used to record vocabulary and grammar on these little pieces of paper. I would then take them home afterwards and transfer the information into my notebook. As this is a book of advice, I should be advising you to go out and buy a small notebook and pen to take it with you to your *intercambios* but that's far too academic. Use serviettes, it's a lot more fun!

Just one more point while we are on the subject of *intercambios* in bars. If you are going to a place where your second language is spoken, don't take a pen. If you have just gasped in horror at this piece of advice, read on for the explanation. If you need to write something down and you don't have a pen or pencil, you will be forced to ask the waiter or the barman if you can borrow one, which means you will be practising your second language and increasing your *ET*!

I went on an *intercambio* once which involved walking around the beautiful Retiro Park in the centre of Madrid. Unfortunately, this was not a good experience for me because, quite simply, I found it difficult to walk and talk! I know it sounds strange but I remember feeling very uncomfortable because I wasn't able to concentrate fully. The reason I had difficulties was probably due to the fact that I had a low level of Spanish at that time but a female friend of mine had another theory, "men are not good at multitasking," she told me with a grin.

I have also tried language exchanges over the internet. These are a great time saver because you don't have to travel anywhere. You simply agree on a time, log on and speak with your *intercambio* friend. From personal experience, I prefer to do this without using video because of my need to concentrate fully by putting my energy into listening but maybe that's because I am a man and I am not good at multitasking, as my friend pointed out to me.

So, what are you waiting for? Start the ball rolling.

EXAMS

If I were to ask you if you would prefer to be relaxing on a beach or to be taking an exam, you would probably give the first option as your answer. If I were to ask you if you would prefer to be in a pit full of snakes or in an exam room, you would probably also give the first option as your answer. So I think it's fair to say that nobody relishes the prospect of sitting an exam. So, why do we put ourselves through them? Why don't we all just go to the beach and relax instead? Before I am held responsible for a mass exodus to the coast, I think I should explain. Exams are a test of our knowledge and abilities and the results are a message to the world of how good or bad we are at a particular subject. If, at this point, we channel our energy into thinking about positive results and how good they make us feel, I am sure we can slowly begin to fall in love with them. If we pass them, the qualifications they provide are our friends for life! So let's embrace them and make them our buddies. Like any new acquaintance, we need to know a little bit more about them.

If you are studying English, the following short section will be of interest to you. If, like me however, you are studying another language, you will have to skip this or make a cup of coffee or head to the nearest beach. If you do go to the beach, please take some sunscreen. You see! This book is full of advice!

- TOEFL – *Test of English as a Foreign Language. (Essential for entry into universities in the U.S.A)*

- TOEIC – *Test of English for International Communication. (Designed to test ability in an international working environment)*

- CAMBRIDGE EXAMS - *KET (Key English Test-A2) PET (Preliminary English Test-B1) FCE (First Certificate in English-B2) CAE (Certificate of Advanced English-C1) CPE (Certificate of Proficiency in English) There are also some business English exams. The qualifications from these exams are recognised by employers, universities and government ministries as proof of level.*

- IELTS – *The International English language Testing System (Developed by Cambridge University in conjunction with The British Council. For people who need to work/study where communication is made in English. Required for universities in the UK)*

- TRINITY – A test of speaking and listening skills *(approved for UK visa or settlement purposes)*

The best place for information regarding exams nowadays is the internet. I say this because there are often changes to keep up with the fast changing pace of the world but also to check prices and available dates. You should decide which exam is right for you and research it accordingly.

As part of the research for this book, I have perused various websites looking for information about the above exams and I have tried some of the online tests. If we bear in mind why the CEFR was set up, I would imagine the tasks in these exams are similar for any language. My results of this investigation are the following. The exams at B2 level are not easy, that is not to say they are super difficult, so I would like to settle on the word *challenging*. So what does this mean? The answer is quite simple. You will not pass these exams if you do not work hard. You simply cannot rely on luck or the good old cheat sheet!

At the time of writing, Spain is just beginning to emerge from a very austere period. At the height of the recession, there were around six million unemployed. During this time, it was not uncommon for me to be giving classes to a room full of people who were without work.

Thankfully, that situation is changing, albeit very slowly. There are job opportunities now but a lot of them require a good level of English. Let's be clear why. It is because most business nowadays is global and English is fast becoming the international business language.

As human beings, we have to be able to adapt to the ever changing world in which we live and if learning a language, be it English or any other language, is essential for our job, we have at some point to sit an exam, to demonstrate our abilities but also to prove to ourselves how wonderful we are for completing a gruelling course of studies! One thing I have learned, however, especially where language studies are concerned, is that you simply cannot skip lower level grammar and fast track yourself to a B2 level exam. It just doesn't work like that for many reasons. Some course books at that level are designed for exam practice and have been written in the belief that the student is familiar with all the grammar up to that stage. There is, of course, the other question of vocabulary. If you have decided to sit a B2 level exam, you should also have a very good knowledge of words. Consider sitting a lower level exam, or several if they are available, as a form of preparation for the higher level exams. If you can produce a pass certificate along with the promise to a potential employer that you fully intend to improve your language abilities, you fully intend to obtain a higher level qualification *and* you smile nicely, you might get the job!

I completely understand that after several years without work, people feel desperate and feel the only option is to throw themselves into a course of studies which is higher than their abilities in order to stand a chance of getting a job but you have to be careful. It can be incredibly personally damaging and demoralising to pay for and then fail an exam because you were not equipped to pass it.

Before you start thinking there is no hope, please remember, there is always hope! I know of many excellent grammar books which will take you from A1 to B2 level. These books contain explanations, practice and answers and can therefore be used at home to supplement your course of studies. I am studying Spanish from a book just like this. Some of the grammar I already know but it's a good idea for me to review certain constructions and also to test myself from time to time. By studying this way, I am also learning new vocabulary and increasing my *ET*. Yes, I'm a good student!

I have no plans to sit a Spanish exam in the near future mainly because I am not under any pressure to do so. Having said that, I would like to do so at some point in time, but only so that I can provide evidence of my level. My main reason for not wanting to take an exam now is because I am not ready to do so. I have estimated my level at B1 and ,although I am happy to have reached that stage, I know that if I were to sit a B2 level exam, I would fail miserably.

The message here is to decide on the exam you want to take, research it thoroughly, find out what you need to do to pass it and then work hard. Be realistic, be honest with yourself and don't waste your time or money chasing something out of reach.

SUBTITLES

Very often, I am asked by my students if they should use subtitles when watching films. I have to say, I find this a difficult subject to advise on. I can give you the benefit of my experience and what I prefer to do when watching films but I can't offer one piece of advice.

One thing I will say is that, if the object of watching a film is to improve your listening skills, the idea of using subtitles seems rather redundant. If we cast our minds back to the four language skills, you will notice that, apart from minimal written language in films where you can practise your reading skills, the only skill possible to practise is listening; writing and speaking are not options.

The problem I have found with films is that because they are visual, it is possible to understand part of the story just by watching. I have also found that after a period of time I begin to lose my concentration and start thinking of other things like writing second language learning advice books. At these moments, I opt for the subtitles in order to understand what is happening.

So we are back to the original dilemma, subtitles or not? One thing I would like to advise against is putting the subtitles in your native language. All this will do is help you understand the story and therefore enjoy the film but it is defeating the object of the exercise and I am sorry to say it doesn't count towards *ET*.

As mentioned earlier in the chapter entitled *Listening*, watch short films on Youtube without subtitles. The videos can be short, so even an easily distracted person such as me will be able to concentrate. You also have the option of watching the video several times until you understand it.

Remember to make a list of all the words you hear and recognise. Watch the same short video several times and try to add more words to the list each time you do.

This type of exercise can often take up as much time as watching a film on TV or DVD but, in my opinion, it is far more beneficial. And you can log the time as *ET*!

REVIEW AND MEMORISE

Even if you make the same mistake thousands of times or you can't remember how to construct a sentence or question, your teacher will help you and will give you more practice or will simply explain the grammar again. A teacher will never refuse to help you because it is his or her responsibility to be patient and continue helping until you are either fluent or you have become so embarrassed by making the same mistakes thousands of times that you have left to find a new teacher!

It is clear, then, that all students will be provided with the necessary information and practice so that they can gain knowledge and improve their skills; *that's the teacher's job*.

However, what a teacher cannot do is commit language to the student's memory; *that's the student's job*.

It is very important to memorise basic classroom language and basic classroom questions. This will involve reviewing your studies regularly and, in the case of basic questions which are fundamental in and out of the classroom, committing them to memory.

So, stop whatever you are doing (unless you are doing your homework) and go do some memorising!

MISTAKES ARE GOOD!

When I have completed my Spanish homework, I present it to my teacher thinking that it is perfect and that I am the best student she has ever had. A short time later, my exercises are covered in red biro. When I experienced this for the first time, I was devastated. I had spent a long time doing the exercises and even longer checking them, only to discover the majority covered in red ink. It is demoralizing but necessary. I have learned a lot from my mistakes and although, sometimes, I continue to make the same errors, I realise it is part of the learning process. The following example is not one of my best but I think you will understand what I am trying to say: If you made the mistake of stroking an aggressive dog and were bitten, would you stroke that dog again? If you have just answered *yes* to that question, I would

94

suggest there is no hope for you. Of course, the answer is no. This means that you have learned a valuable lesson due to your mistake.

CORRECTIONS

Very often I have found it almost impossible to correct a mistake because I simply can't grasp what I am supposed to do. When this happens, I ask my teacher or a Spanish speaking friend for help. If this happens to you, you should do the same. Under no circumstances should you copy from another student. Discovering the answer with help from a third party will be far more gratifying than correcting by copying. Look at it this way: You have worked very hard to complete an exercise and have made a few mistakes; if you copy, you are giving up. Imagine running 25 miles of a marathon and deciding to stop because you couldn't face the final mile. The message here is to find a way to achieve the results that you deserve.

HANDHELD DEVICES

More than ever before, modern life provides us with many devices and gadgets to make our lives much easier than life in the past. I am old enough to remember seeing queues of people waiting outside telephone boxes many years ago because they couldn't afford a private telephone at home. If you are reading this and you are under twenty, you are probably thinking that a telephone box is the packaging that your smart phone came in. How wrong you are! Nowadays, most people have a mobile phone of which a large number are probably smart phones. I love mine and in my opinion it is the ultimate gadget. I am amazed when I think of the unending possibilities this technology has to offer me in the palm of my hand. One of those possibilities is to choose from an enormous range of languages. You can probably see where

I am going with this. OK, it is obvious, but you need to change the language on your phone to your *SL*. Think about how often you look at your trusty friend. If you were to add up the time I am sure it would surprise you how long you could spend exposing your eyes to your second language. And don't forget that if you are performing tasks and following instructions using that language, this can be counted towards your *ET*.

But let's not stop there. If you haven't done it already, change the language on your computer, your tablet, your car radio, your microwave, the cash machine at your bank and any other device or gadget that allows this option. When you buy a train ticket from one of those touch screen machines, choose your second language.

WHAT HAPPENS IN THE CLASSROOM
STAYS IN THE CLASSROOM

When you visit the doctor and explain the medical problems that you have, you expect him or her to be discreet. I believe the same rules of discretion should apply in the classroom. I have a strict policy regarding this. Basically, what I hear or see in the classroom stays in the classroom.

It's almost impossible to give classes to students, especially on a one to one basis, without finding out things about their personal or professional lives. On a daily basis, I can be exposed to business information which a company would rather keep confidential. I am sometimes made aware of other people's illnesses without their knowledge and I have also had to deal with students breaking down due to severe problems in their personal lives. But you will notice that I haven't mentioned any names and never will do. Discretion is very important. I am sure that most teachers feel the same but it is important for you, the student, to follow suit.

Very often when learning a language, you can find yourself talking about a subject because that is the only associated vocabulary you can think of at that moment. And because you are using your second language, it might not have occurred to you that information you wouldn't normally talk about so freely in your own language has been divulged. This is understandable and I have done it myself in Spanish classes but I have felt comfortable enough to speak about personal matters because of this unwritten discretion rule.

So, remember please.

What happens in the classroom stays in the classroom!

Made in the USA
Charleston, SC
30 April 2015